THIS

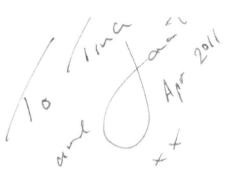

THIS IS IT

THE ART OF HAPPILY GOING NOWHERE

MAURICE FULLARD SMITH

DARTON · LONGMAN + TODD

First published in 2007 by
Darton, Longman and Todd Ltd
1 Spencer Court
140–142 Wandsworth High Street
London SW18 4JJ

ISBN–10 0–232–52693–1
ISBN–13 978–0–232–52693–6

A catalogue record for this book is available from the
British Library.

Designed and produced by Sandie Boccacci
Printed and bound in Great Britain by
The Cromwell Press, Trowbridge, Wiltshire

Contents

CONTENTS

Acknowledgements

With my thanks to George Tarleton for pointing me in the right direction, Alan Haldan for continued inspiration, Dave Bryant whose songs have been a light in dark places, Bridget Boyle for unlimited helpful advice and practical assistance, and Brendan Walsh for seeing so much potential in the manuscript.

On my pilgrimage towards enlightenment I owe a great debt to my family and to many friends for their patience and understanding with my undulating mental and emotional condition. I would also like to acknowledge the considerable life-changing insights received through the writings of Anthony de Mello and Eckhart Tolle.

Not least I would like to thank the kind benefactors – who would not wish to be named – who have believed in Eileen and me when many others could not understand the path we were treading. You have made a great difference to our lives.

Introduction

The seemingly precocious title of this book –
This Is It – is not meant to suggest that within
these pages lies the complete answer to the
problems of our troubled minds and our
troubled world. Rather, it is another voice
extolling the virtue of stillness, and it is
inspired by the intriguing mystic saying, *'This
is it; nothing happens next.'* It is a voice that is
grateful for all the other voices – like the
sound of many waters swelling with one state
of awareness – drawing us into the present
moment, which have contributed to my
ability to embrace life as it is and to live at
peace in the here and now.

As you read you may come across a few
words or expressions that are not part of your
normal vocabulary. It may be helpful to pause
to let them impress you. Such words can be a
valuable means of clarifying what is happening to you, or if pondered quietly, they

may open doors into a deeper and fuller dimension of living. The words have been born out of experience; pausing in their presence can prevent us from adopting them as mere concepts in our minds. Letting these words sink in, slowly and consciously, often allows them to change our lives. Pausing deliberately to discover silence and space can be the beginning of living life at a different tempo.

The chapters of this book are short so that you may read just one and then leave time between that and the next to allow the words to remain with you. Each chapter is intended to make something happen within you and is probably best read slowly, leaving gaps between the sentences and, indeed, sometimes even between the words. I have become increasingly convinced that pausing is an art form that allows great changes to develop within us.

Above all, please do not struggle or try hard to understand anything; rather, relax and let everything come to you as a free gift when the time is right. Whoever you are, I wish you well and trust that the time you spend in these pages will be both enjoyable and beneficial.

Maurice Fullard Smith

PART ONE

GET A LIFE!

We already have a life; the trouble is, we often don't like the life we have got. However, our life situation remains, and whatever we may think ... *this is it*. And it will not go away.

All our suffering finds its source here. Pain we may not be able to avoid, but suffering we certainly can. Our unhappiness springs from a non-acceptance of things as they are at this very moment. This can be one of the most difficult facts for us to face, or even consider; but face it we must if we are ever to cease from continual striving and enjoy contentment and peace.

Many years ago I can remember asking for directions from an elderly man in the street. You can imagine my astonishment when he scratched his head before declaring sadly, 'Sorry, you can't get there from here!' This absurd phrase niggled away at me for many years. Where on earth did he expect me to start from, other than where I was?

Thankfully, the man was wrong. His long life had not brought him wisdom. We most certainly can get to a satisfactory destination from our present position. In fact, we cannot get there from anywhere else.

It is our failure to accept where we are, constantly wishing we were out of our present situation, projecting our minds into a past paradise or an imagined ideal future, that prevents us from living now and taking the steps forward that we often long to take.

Now can be the moment for us to stop and to realise that life is as it is. Our constant search for something or somewhere better is delaying our enjoyment of this present moment. And this present moment is all we have. Life is always now.

Many might contend that this present moment is not always enjoyable; but we must not allow ourselves to be drawn into mere semantics, for what I mean by enjoyment is not a constant ecstatic experience, but a deep-seated sense of contentment and peace, whatever our circumstances.

16

GOING NOWHERE

The irony of our journey through life is that there really is nowhere to go. There is no destination that is not where we already are. As many a sage has commented, 'The journey *is* the goal.'

What I am saying is that everything we need is already within us and that our journey is really a discovery of who we are and what we already have. In that sense we are going nowhere. There is no physical place called the Kingdom of Heaven, Nirvana or the Promised Land for us to find. They are in another dimension – they are a condition, not a destination – and they are within us awaiting our discovery.

Imagine for a second what it would be like to have everything we need to be perfectly content. Well, that is how it is when we are free from worries and the ambition to be better off in some way than we are now. We do not have to go anywhere or get anything to improve our condition. All our searching can only lead us to find that the treasure was at home, within us, all the time.

As we consider the way to this happy condition, we shall find that the route is not marked out clearly, step by step. More than likely we shall meander, like a river. Maybe we will even seem to be lost at times. Unlike the man-made systems of canals and reservoirs, our river refuses to be imprisoned within the confines of our expectations. Often our impatient but well-intentioned short cuts will lengthen our journey, and at other times we will make great advances seemingly without any effort at all. On our journey we will learn to live with enigma and paradox. The river will not be hurried or confined.

Stay with it, as we start to take time out to listen to the silence around us and allow ourselves to be spoken to. This means abiding in a place of unknowing, where – by being weak and vulnerable enough to need strengthening from within – we discover a river continually supplying all that we need to reach the goal of

self-realisation. Meanwhile be quietly assured
that all is well … just undiscovered.

PLEASE BE STILL

Stillness of mind is all that is required for us to experience the wonder of living.

For most of us that continuous state does not happen in one glorious moment – although it has been known by some, especially after a 'long, dark night of the soul', when they reach the place where life is just not worth living any more. Such folk sometimes just give up, flop back and go with the flow. They accept their lot and, surprisingly, gain an alluring twinkle in their eyes that betrays the secret of those who realise that they cannot solve or avoid their problems and those of society at large. They have left the mad pursuit of modern riches and have ceased to be obsessed with being successful. 'Getting on' – an oft-repeated expression that has robbed our generation of genuine satisfaction – no longer interests them. They accept that life is not fair and do not complain about it.

I am referring not only to the pursuit of material possessions, but also to the whole wretched belief that better health, another location, a new spouse, or some situation other than that in which we now find ourselves, will bring us the continual peace and happiness we are searching for. It may well be the time for us to move to a different home, to change our job situation, or whatever – but let us not fool ourselves that this will be the panacea for all ills. It just seems the right time for a change, and so we do it. We shall take life as it comes, without demanding that everything works out as we hoped it would. Things are different, that is all.

This list of things we feel we need to make us happy often includes the desire to have answers to all our questions, and this is a major stumbling-block for many. The idea that answered questions or a change in our circumstances will automatically bring satisfaction is a lie – perhaps the biggest and most successful lie ever told, and one that has almost totally misled much of the world for centuries.

Maybe this is a good time to stop reading for a moment and to ponder what I am saying. That is a most rewarding habit to develop. I am not suggesting some really deep thinking, accompanied by a furrowed brow; but just a pause, a still moment for the impact of the following statement to really sink in:

Having answers to all our questions or improving our life situation does not guarantee lasting satisfaction.

Being unhappy in luxury is not a fulfilling life-style. Moving to the sun does not mean the end of all our problems. Stillness of mind is a much greater treasure. If we can avoid judging this matter instantly – if we can delay making an immediate decision about whether it is right or wrong, good or bad, by just leaving it on the shelf for now – then our true inner-self may start to arise and speak to us. A whole new way of living begins to emerge.

Can we just let this statement *be?* We could say this is listening with our whole being, our whole person, not just our mind.

For many, this is the beginning of being wise, rather than collecting yet more knowledge or information for our memory bank.

Stillness of mind, not new answers or circumstances, brings peace.

I am convinced that most of us need to face this issue – of where our satisfaction really comes from – before we can find lasting peace and contentment.

Now let some time pass. Perhaps much time.

I will not say 'Be patient', because patience is in very short supply these days. But let us call it 'letting time pass' – a phrase used to great effect by the saintly Dr Claire Weekes, who helped so many agoraphobia sufferers in her lifetime.

These could be our first *very still moments*, living above the mind and feeling fully alive, even if only for a few seconds or, perhaps, minutes. There are no thoughts in our mind;

we are still. However short the time, let us be encouraged. It is a start, and that is the important thing. By going nowhere we are really moving!

THE POWER OF WEAKNESS

Thankfully, there are some magic words that can help us, even though words are so often a poor form of communication that can lead us into a labyrinth of pathways in the mind. Nevertheless, sometimes they can cause a spark of illumination that leads to great things.

Words such as *let*, *allow* or *permit* are kind, passive words that mean we are causing something to happen without making any effort, except perhaps just relaxing. Surely that must sound attractive to anyone who is tired of the continual forced pace of modern living. To many they may sound weak words, especially to those whose ego urges them to be strong, forceful, go-getting personalities; but to those who hunger and thirst for the restfulness that constantly eludes them, these words are a breath of hope.

The power of weakness has been grossly

ignored. What we are considering here is not about allowing ourselves to be trampled underfoot by all and sundry, but about recognising that there is a power at work within us which will work wonders for us if we relax and let it flow through us. Such recognition requires the simple admission that we did not create ourselves and that the essential, basic necessities of life are provided and are happening to us without our aid. Breathing is the prime example.

Take a moment aside now, please. I really do mean *now* – this very minute, please. Just allow a few very long moments to pass as you realise that …

You … are … being … breathed.

A higher power is at work in and around you. All this is happening without fuss and noise. Stay still. For this moment there is peace.

Taking a few more moments now and again to simply observe this constant miracle happening to you, could prove to be one of the most rewarding steps you ever take towards all that you have hoped for – the time when things begin to work for you instead of seemingly being in constant conflict with you.

Living a happy life is no more difficult than letting ourselves breathe. Once the realisation dawns that everything does not depend upon us, we start consciously *just being here now*, instead of constantly doing, doing, doing. There is no need to fill every moment. You can be still. Do not be afraid of inactivity. Any necessary doing will come in due course, but then it will arise out of your stillness and inner peace. This will bring an end to all the havoc that ensues from our restless impetuosity. In fact our action will be all the more effective, as it will now come from our true, innermost source as we let, allow or permit time to pass.

THE GENTLE ART OF FLOATING

Floating through life – that is another way of expressing what we are learning, and it could not be simpler. If we relax and lie still in the water, we will float. But often we hear folk sadly declare that they cannot swim. They are trying to run before they can walk, or to swim before they first start to float.

I do not know of any more pleasant experience than floating, lying on my back and being taken along by the current. Although at one time I was a contender for the world worrying championship, I found it almost impossible to participate when lying on my back floating along. It was many years before I was ready to lie back in everyday life, to accept myself as I was, to float and enjoy the fruits of stillness.

Floating through life may seem like an impossible dream to you at this moment, but more and more people are realising this impossible dream, even when engaged in the most strenuous of activities. I well remember hearing the husband and coach of Joyce Smith, the first winner of the women's London Marathon, calling out to her as she stretched away into the lead, 'Float, Joyce, float!' He knew what he was talking about.

Today on a TV programme I heard Dame Kelly Holmes say that she found herself running even faster as she realised she had won her second Olympic gold medal and automatically relaxed. This was yards before she reached the tape! Life is there, as a ready teacher, if we are ready to hear.

Often we cannot hear and relax until we have striven so hard that we are forced to give up such strenuous effort. We won't let go until we can't hang on any longer. We struggle and strive until we are eventually ready to have our final disappointment with ourselves. Collapsed into failure – or lack of satisfaction even with our success – we are ready to hear the wisdom of the ages that was locked up inside us all the time: relax, accept, you are perfectly all right as you are. In the race of life we can all be winners if we learn the gentle art of floating.

Once again, let us take this moment to pause and start our floating experience.

If you want to do so, then you may lie down on the floor or on your bed, or you can sit erect in a chair, dignified, but not rigid.

Drop your shoulders now and relax with a gentle sigh.

Be aware of your breathing again.

If it helps, you can say quietly, 'Life is as it is ... life is as it is', to the rhythm of your breath.

Stay relaxed and afloat like this for as long as you feel comfortable.

Don't struggle to empty your mind.

If troubling thoughts come to disturb you, don't engage with them, but just observe them.

Let the unwanted thoughts come.

They can be like small puffy clouds going across the sky.

Watch them come and go.

Someone said these thoughts are to him like a parade marching past that he can just watch and smile at.

He doesn't need to follow the brass band.

This is how life can be when we are floating effortlessly along.

It is a taste of heaven, and it will increase as we practise being present in the here and now – observing, observing.

We are not ambitious, but accepting whatever progress we make, fast or slow.

Trying to float causes us to sink.

But we are not trying, just being still, aware of our body, our arms and our legs.

We feel heavy and yet we float.
We do not pass judgement.
This moment is as it is, just as
it is.
We are very consciously here,
feeling alert but relaxed.

We do not rush from our floating experience,
but carry some of the peace with us as we
move into our daily tasks. If possible, we
remain aware of the things we are doing, even
seemingly mundane activities like walking up
and down stairs or washing our hands. We are
quietly buying back each moment and are
consciously alive.

NO PERFORMANCE ORIENTATION

Hearing the statement that we are *all right as we are* can be liberating news.

Billy Joel sang his way into my heart with the famous lyric, 'Don't go changing, to try and please me, I love you just the way you are.' Trying to change ourselves, gritting our teeth and embarking upon some great self-improvement crusade, can make us appear quite obnoxious to those suffering even a mild exposure to this self-righteous approach. What warms the parts that effort cannot reach – and often affects those around us too – is to observe the effortless change that comes with a *transformation* from within.

The transformation I am talking about is the process that thrills all those who have learned to trust their innermost life, even in the fires of their most dire life situations. Transformation comes to those who know how to lean inwards, especially when tempted to hold themselves together, or to escape by chasing hotfoot after outer emotional or physical rewards at the expense of inner calm. Such ability is often gained by painful experience, for it is not many who can readily hear the truth that our apparent strengths are often our weaknesses or vulnerable points, while those things that we see as our weaknesses can in fact lead us into strength. The statement, 'When I am weak, then I am strong', has been proved millions of times since a follower of Jesus first uttered it two thousand years ago.

What a relief to realise that our seeming disqualifications could turn out to be the very qualifications that guide our ship of life into the harbour of rest and enjoyment. If we begin to acknowledge that we cannot conquer situations without reference to the eternal stream of Life within us, it indicates that we are falling back into dependence upon the One Life that is flowing from the creative source of all Being. Often we then find – perhaps while floundering once again at our wits' end – that we have coped better than we could ever have imagined possible.

When we make such a weak and dependent condition our permanent residence, we gradually notice a latent power springing up within us that develops into a constant stream of effortless ability. Watched and nurtured by quiet appreciation, this stream will finally turn into a river in full spate, carrying all our cares away with it. This is the fulfilling life we have been searching for. Dependence upon a higher power will transform us into strong, independent people who are unself-consciously pointing the way to the highway of happiness.

Aims and goals, targets and great incentives, may have their place in the madly competitive world of sport, business or politics, where rewards are short-lived and, indeed, often bring disguised unhappiness with them. When we are considering the realm of ultimate satisfaction, inner peace or sublime joy, such methods are woefully inadequate. Our performance will not help us here. This is where we need to be utterly reliant upon the unfailing power that is within us – which in fact *is us*, as we realise when we are finally seeing aright. God is our true life. The Force *is* with us. We are OK as we are.

We cannot all be business tycoons, world champions or leaders of nations … and we are not aiming to be better at being still than anyone else! We are just enjoying being fully alive *in this moment*, whatever our circumstances. We are finding fulfilment in the pastures of inner transformation as we accept who, what and where we are. At source, we are all wonderful people who have temporarily lost our way in a mad world of competition.

We can take the first step back to sanity *now* by being silent for a moment and allowing a still, small voice to whisper that …

We are unique and acceptable as we are.

Let us allow the truth of that statement to permeate our whole body as we sit where we are, for just a few more moments.

A CASE OF MISTAKEN IDENTITY

Who are we really? I suppose this question has been rattling around the minds of intellectuals for more years than we could ever imagine. Yet there are very few we meet who seem to have discovered their true identity. We might notice that a high proportion of these contented souls are quite happy with their lot and seem to be simple folk; perhaps they have not even considered the question of who they really are. Maybe many intellectuals are unable to be simple and are not in the truest sense intelligent. Certainly, those who work alongside such cerebral people often speak of their lack of common sense or their inability to live sensibly. They are so often on a mind trip where knowledge and wisdom are revealed time and again as seemingly incompatible twins.

Our schools and colleges have been

feeding the minds of children and adolescents with a constant stream of facts, and these are usually allied to the subjects that are deemed most necessary for success in our wealth- and celebrity-worshipping society. Retention of information has replaced loving instruction in how to live, how to be satisfied with who we are – whatever our IQ, the sum of our possessions, the level of our physical attractiveness or the state of our health. The ideal of satiation has replaced that of satisfaction; while simplicity, the breeding ground of true happiness, has been largely overlooked.

Declaring, as so many do, '*I am not myself* today', indicates that we often speak without realising what we are saying. The true 'I' has never been the 'myself' as seen by those around me. We have failed to understand that at heart we are all intrinsically wonderful people; we are not just the expression of behaviour that is the result of our heredity or environmental upbringing. We are much more than that! Such a liberating insight was never taught in any school or college I have encountered; yet knowing who we are *in essence* is foundational for a truly successful and contented life.

Hidden away beneath our constant flood of thoughts, feelings and actions is a pure river of life, a perfect person or super-being, constituted to be absolutely suitable to live out our span here, free of inner disturbance, noise and anxiety. It is this pure stream we need to locate and nurture if we are to be fulfilled on our journey through life. If we start to tell children how wonderful they are, then we will begin to see the emergence of the true life they were meant to live. They will start to love themselves without a trace of narcissism. Surely in this respect we should all become like little children again – prepared to unlearn so much that ambition and sophistication have taught us and to become simple people again.

Once we start to realise how intrinsically wonderful we are, then our narcissistic habits and our constant concern with matters like appearances and self-importance, gradually start to fade away. Our insecurities are being dealt the first of many death-blows and we

are on the happy pathway of inner transformation again. We are growing up into an
awareness of who we really are.

TIME TO STAND
AND STARE

Having gained a glimpse of the fact that we are intrinsically wonderful, maybe we can now stop judging everything we say and do. More importantly, perhaps, can we stop weighing every thought that comes uninvited into our busy minds, and become a quiet observer? Pausing to watch our thoughts and the world go by can mark the beginning of a holy habit that will become the richest attribute we can ever possess. It will be a million times more satisfying in the long term than winning a fortune in the national lottery. We have made contact with the Eternal, the timeless stream of a peaceful Life that has been patiently and unobtrusively waiting to enjoy our company.

If we can do this, even momentarily, it means we have separated ourselves from the person we wrongly believe ourselves to be. It

ₙne first step towards detachment – a happy
state indeed.

*The real you is the one who is
doing the observing.*

The other 'person' is an impostor, a masque-
rading bundle of thoughts, memories and
projections who constantly refuses to come
into line and accept that our life situation is as
it is now.

I suppose a psychologist might label this
constant nuisance, this ever-repeating story in
our minds, our 'Ego'. I see it as 'the Beast that
runs amok in my forehead', but that is too
wordy and gives him too much credit, so I'll
choose a simpler name and put him in his
place. I will call him 'Silly Me'. All that Silly
Me wants is attention, not caring whether that
attention is comforting or painful. He is quite
ready to laugh or cry or show a stiff upper lip,
quite content to strut or cringe, so long as he
(or she) does not have to be the servant of the
deepest realm of our Being.

'Me' is not content to listen to the innermost 'I' – as some have explained the matter when trying to put the almost inexplicable into words. There seems a constant warfare between the inner mind-person and the *innermost* person, or spirit, which is the One Life permeating our creation, currently wanting to be expressed uniquely through each of us to the common good.

Trying to curb or improve the usurping mind-person is to fight fire with fire. We are giving him or her more attention, and that is just what he or she craves. All we need do is *observe without judgement*, and the separation is made. We look and live. There is stillness and silence in our minds. For a moment the warfare has ceased and we experience peace. We naturally rejoice when we first experience this, if only for a moment or two, for it is indeed true bliss. We have stopped judging something, we have viewed it dispassionately for a moment, and we have reaped a magnanimous reward. We may then begin to realise that we have spent our whole life judging ourselves and judging others without noticing that we were doing it. Dissecting and examining each encounter with every person and event kills the sense of pure presence that is the essence of inner peace.

Of course, our ego will not give up without a fight. Bombarding us with continual thoughts is its major means of assault. Not thinking, being silent and still, is death to ego's existence. We learn not to be ignorant of such devices, and the day soon comes when we may be surprised to find a gentle chuckle rising up within us, as we realise we have been caught out yet again. Thankfully, we have begun to take ourselves less seriously, realising that once more we were trapped in a wasteful mind-exercise, unbidden thoughts madly following each other and proving unrewarding, as ever.

We should mark such an occasion as a red-letter day, for it heralds the approach of a reign of increasing peace and contentment. I clearly recall the moment I first sat by the river of life and heard it chuckle (what a delightful word that is), and it was at a very sad period in my life situation.

Chuckling has always appealed to me. It

can be a very healthy experience, in addition to bringing pure enjoyment. Why not stand and stare at nothing in particular for a while, perhaps allowing yourself a small grin? Who knows what it will lead to?

DYING BEFORE YOU DIE

I am acutely aware of the many people I have known who cannot enter into a restful and enjoyable state of living because it all sounds too easy. Indeed, this was my own difficulty for a very long time. We are so used to attainment by effort that the mere thought of receiving everything as a free gift rings alarm bells. Indeed, some folk find it hard to receive anything at all without a struggle. As for doing absolutely nothing to deserve what they get, that can be anathema.

We have all met those who are so busy serving others that they will not let anyone serve them; they cannot receive. This is a particular folly found among some religious societies, where we are often made painfully aware of how much we are being helped. Some folk cannot even deliver a simple glass of water without drawing so much attention that we wonder if we are being served champagne. How refreshing it is when matters are quietly and efficiently attended to without being noticed, or when someone prefers to just sit with us, rather than fuss around doing things we don't really need done.

Our daily situations are often full of hard knocks and the road may at times seem unbearable, even beyond our powers of endurance. But when we have abdicated the responsibility to cope ably, no matter what the cost to our pride, then we are ready to discover the internal source that is ever waiting to take the strain and stress out of our lives. Even hardship becomes easy when grace is at work. There is no room for boasting in our abilities when this is how we live. Our ego has taken another death-blow. We have 'lost our life', yet strangely gained it again.

Death is what we are talking about. Not a subject that many like to embrace, but death is our entrance into life in all its abundance. Dying before we die – before we finally experience our physical death – will not sound a very attractive proposition if we are determined to maintain our strong opinions, or if we need to appear to be in complete control and are highly concerned for our image. To those who are tired of keeping up appearances and are prepared to learn to die, the relief is inestimable.

We no longer have to present a triumphant front once we are aware of the power that is at work within us.

This power emerges without a fanfare when we abdicate the number-one spot and embrace our extreme weakness.

Why don't we just sit quietly in the presence of this statement before moving on to the next chapter?

THE END OF THE STRUGGLE

Death itself is weakness at its most extreme, nothing to be afraid of. The peaceful look we see on the faces of some people during their last moments on earth is often there because they have finally given up the struggle to live. For many this is the first time they have ever given up fighting their difficult situations, particularly if they were taught from a young age always to cope triumphantly, to be tough, never to cry, and other stoic follies so admired by many people.

I have spent much time in recent years quietly welcoming death. It is not a morbid or unpleasant occupation. Our physical dying may be painful, but death itself is a natural part of our journey; in fact it is almost the only thing we can be sure of after drawing our first breath. Although I have not taken up the Eastern mystic practice of sitting for hours among the tombs, I can understand why they do it. They are acquainting themselves with death, because the fear of death, in one form or another, reduces our lives to one long continual struggle.

Every ending – or mini-death – I have experienced has led eventually to an increase in some other form; so I am encouraged to trust that the final experience will prove no exception. (This is not an attempt to convince you there is life after our physical death, for the holding of strong spiritual beliefs is a hindrance that has, thankfully, dropped off me along the way. Ideological belief-systems can easily lead to acrimonious disagreements and even horrendous warfare, as we are all currently aware. I prefer to say that I only know what I have experienced and do not argue the matter further.)

If we are experiencing situations we do not like and can do nothing about, then we have the option to face the truth of this. It is as it is. Then we can consciously relax our bodies rather than struggle in our minds. We are beginning to accept things as they are *now*, even if we decide to make a change of some sort in the future! We need to 'die' to this business of continually wanting this moment to improve.

We can trust the true Life at our centre to do the best in every situation. In this way we become 'dead' to oughts and shoulds, free from continually acting out of duty and the obligation to constantly do good deeds – and indeed, free from the impulse to turn mere temptation into evil deeds! The appropriate action will arise within us, if and when needed, without any struggle. We delight to find that we do not have a liar, a thief, a murderer or a self-righteous do-gooder living at our centre. Our life becomes spontaneous and quietly thrilling as we observe our transformation from within. Acceptance brings peace, and peace precedes our unhurried and most appropriate action.

Eventually our whole egocentric self is undermined and we just don't care what life throws at us. It is as it is. Not that we are anaesthetised – some pain comes to us all – but self-induced suffering ceases as our extreme weakness, our dependence or mini-death, inexorably leads to more and more acceptance. Once we have exhausted our-selves of all attempts to be adequate and to cope, then total acceptance *comes* – we can't force this – bringing with it an automatic transformation to our lives. Gradually every-thing begins to appear perfect, or as it should be for us right now. The pressure is off; a sense of peace has arrived.

Recognising our inability to be all-conquering heroes, then yielding into our weakness instead of fighting our trials valiantly, allows the latent majestic power within each of us to come shining through:

> There's a life inside you which can't be beat,
> And when you find it you'll be on your feet ...

So wrote a song-writer friend of mine many years ago. Let us lean inwards into that Inner Life now, whatever our situation, and 'let time pass'. We are not looking for anything to change – not even our feelings. We are still.

LIFE IS A DANCE

A dance may be the last thing you imagine life to be, especially if you feel you have lead in your boots. Yet our heavy afflictions can seem light once the music of divine enabling is coursing through our veins.

Not all music is ragtime and most of us tire of constant hilarity. The jester who never takes a break becomes wearisome. So the melody and rhythm of our dance of life may change as events buffet us badly or, alternatively, as they bring us obvious pleasure; but once we have learned even the slightest trace of acceptance, we find there is still some joy shining through, even in our sorrows. We have not become stoics – far from it – but those with a lightness of foot, moving to a melody we never expected to hear. We are in tune with the heart of the universe that knows both darkness and light.

I am not suggesting that we should dance

53

in order to make ourselves happy, but that we are dancing inside because we are basically content, whatever the melody or the rhythm we hear. Cheering ourselves up is a very profitless exercise, a fire that needs constant stoking; yet it is the advice continually offered by those who have never been still inside long enough to hear the strains of comfort being played by an unseen orchestra. Such words do not help our cause.

All this may seem metaphoric if we are still wanting relief from physical pain or demanding material wealth in exchange for our poverty. For those determined to find their solution in Vanity Fair, this is not what they want to hear, but those who are weary of quick-fix answers and need a good long rest are perhaps just beginning to catch the stirrings of a love song that has been there all the time. It has been unheard amid the mind-noise that accompanies the mad rush to get somewhere other than where we are, or to be someone other than who we are.

There *is* a place of quiet rest where pure enjoyment reigns, a place where the music never ceases to be available. We may be too old or too infirm to physically dance, yet there is no need for us to become wallflowers; our eyes can dance and light up the room, even though sometimes through our tears.

Over forty years ago two very elderly gentlemen – one a cultured merry old fellow with a twinkle in his eyes, the other a sad old man but with no complaint in his eyes – both helped turn my feet towards the path of constant contentment, whatever my circumstances might be … and neither of them said a word. They were dancing to the same conductor, but to very different melodies.

I love the words 'quietness' and 'confidence'. They may sound like two very different tunes, but they harmonise perfectly when they are orchestrated by our acceptance of the vicissitudes of our life here on earth. Seen together in one person, they constitute the most beautiful music. They do not come to everyone, and may be unwelcome because many mistake 'quiet confidence' for missing out, thinking that loquacity and assertiveness are the necessary assets for success. That may be so, if by success we mean recognition by others, or pecuniary or material gain; but, hopefully, by now we are at least beginning to see that these are not the golden assets that we deep-down long for, however much they glitter and catch our attention.

Quiet confidence is a major strength that emerges with time in those who have learned to dance in the schools of weakness and acceptance. Such people are rarely applauded openly, although many secretly admire them, for in today's society it is not 'cool' to appreciate such an attitude. I am not suggesting that our personalities should be flattened out so we all become alike. Those of us with unbiased eyes and ears will catch the sense of these inner virtues, whether we are observing those who quickly indulge in riotous dance steps or those who prefer to 'sit this one out'.

All dancers prove engaging once they are dancing to an inner tune.

PART TWO

WHEN DARKNESS COMES

The onset of unexpected depression, described variously by sufferers as a black hole, a black dog, or utter pointlessness, can bring a sense of devastation altering the pattern of our lives beyond recognition. Friends may wonder what on earth is happening to us and may be completely unable to empathise, for it seems to them quite impossible to get oneself into such distress.

The problem is all the more confusing if we have been flying pretty high, with no sign of an oncoming storm. In fact, for many, being too 'high' often does precede a descent into a cloud of heaviness that threatens to ruin every thread of progress we have experienced. We don't need a degree in psychology, genetics or environmental science, but it will be useful to have a simple understanding of the best approach we can have to such a distressing condition.

At a time like this, we also find that anxiety can easily come upon us, as hormones flood our body to enable us to fight the darkness, or else to flee from it into some absorbing activity. For many this anxiety seriously compounds the situation. Some of us who have trodden this dark road discovered that there is no way to overcome the devouring monster by will-power. We are forced to give up all attempts to escape as we observe our apparent progress slipping away from us time and time again, leaving us exhausted – just like John Bunyan's Pilgrim in his dungeon of despair.

Accepting the darkness and letting ourselves be overwhelmed by it may sound a dangerous approach to our nearest and dearest, but we find no alternative. If there is a secret of success, probably it is to stay willingly in this dungeon of darkness, just simply realising we have no other option. Although we may hate it, this place is also a part of our journey. Allowing ourselves to fully experience the presence of these terrible moments is a major step forward, although we may not recognise it as such at the time.

Going *consciously* into our dark times, feeling them fully and so turning the weight of their presence into a floating experience, can eventually be the catalyst that causes a little light to begin to seep into our dark night. This transmutation cannot be hurried, nor can it be accomplished by repeating a purely cerebral formula or concept. The beginning of change is often the result of our genuine surrender to a black situation that is present in this very moment of time. Our long-term plans are put on hold as we constantly relax back into the power of the present moment.

As we accept and relax in our discomfort, it is a great help to remember not to identify with the depression and anxiety. It is not who we intrinsically are, but grounded in the lake of sorrow or body of pain that our ego has built up during our personal history and even in our genetic background. We can observe this condition as we have learned to do with unwanted thoughts. We are not trying to change anything by will-power. We are detached.

61

Maybe for some there will be a very long period of such mental and emotional (we could even say spiritual) pain, but we shall not struggle to escape. We do not like our situation, but here we are, accepting it. Once again, *this is it*. There is no escape. We are not simply wallowing in self-pity, as some may think. We are exhausted.

For many of us – again like Pilgrim – our acceptance may finally herald a day when we discover that the golden key to the dungeon was in our pocket all the time. We have learned more deeply than ever, whatever condition we are in, to be content. A cautious sigh of relief would probably not go amiss at this point on the road.

I will not attempt a deep explanation of the purpose of such experiences, and I do not claim to be an expert in medical knowledge of the matter. Neither do I speak lightly, for in extreme cases we are speaking of a condition that has led many to a final despair. But I do know from experience that the insights we have shared often lead to hope and inner transformation that, at one time, seemed impossible.

As time passes we come to realise how the timbre of our lives has been radically enhanced through the experiences we have endured. We shall never be the people we were. There is a new depth of peace and understanding within us, as we move on from our black night into the dawn of a new day.

WE ARE NEVER ALONE

As we continue our exploration of the mystery of life, there may come a time when we are shocked to realise that even moving into stillness has become a subtle effort. We are caught *trying* again. This seeming disappointment gradually opens yet another door to further fulfilment, the beginning of *always living with a sense of presence*.

This will probably come when we have sought till we have no more strength to seek, and for us the search for truth is now really over – even the search for greater stillness. For some this acceptance may come after a long journey through life. However, when such insight does settle within us, the discoveries will not cease, but we will know for certain that the seeking has come to an end. Everything now will feel serendipitous, but is in fact a continual gift of grace.

Perhaps, as in my own experience, this

will come when we are being as still as we can be, yet the mind never gives up, but continues to plague us until we are fooled yet again into trying to disperse our thoughts with stillness. Then one day, maybe quite surprisingly, we realise that we are past caring at all about the mind-noise and are able to see right through it and let it be. Now even this nuisance *is as it is*. Everything is. As 'seeing through' all appearances becomes a habit, we are filled with joy, ever embracing in a deeper and deeper way the truth that the Presence is always with us. We don't have to get rid of anything to find the continual peace that we have previously experienced in such paucity.

Suddenly our living takes on a new dimension. We are constantly aware that the stillness is not only with us, but is our very essence and can never leave us. The mind-noise has not driven the Presence away, only diverted us and nullified our consciousness of the eternal commitment. Once this insistent ego-manoeuvre is exposed, we shall no longer fight, or even be disturbed by intrusive thoughts. We shall quietly and confidently

smile our way through them as our consciousness increases and we rejoice in the fact that
we have never been forsaken for a moment
and are never alone. The persistent thoughts
will also fade out of existence, even though
we didn't object to their interference.

Thankfully, there will not be an over-
whelming sense of divine Presence at all
times, making us appear other-worldly. But
only a gentle breath or a pause away is all the
fullness of satisfaction we have ever desired.
We shall probably feel constrained to stop in
our tracks every once in a while, just to stand
and appreciate the treasure that is within us.
To say we have bated breath might not be an
exaggeration.

Unwanted desires now start to shrivel up
without a shred of self-denial. We have all we
need – in fact, we always have had – but now
our awareness has grown to the point where
we continually recognise the wonder of the
life that has been breathed into us. We walk on
hallowed ground (but not *over*-consciously,
please), seeing with new eyes and accepting
the same life in everyone and in everything

we encounter. It is often unrecognised, but it is there. We increasingly find we just cannot pass judgement any more, for our own progress has all been without our self-effort; it has been the upsurge of the Inner Energy that is a gracious gift shared by the Source of all Being.

We have discovered the treasure of greatest price buried within the field of our own being. We are one with God now and forever. If the God-word proves troublesome for us, we can just interpret it as an acronym for the 'Great Other Dimension'. However, for many it is important. Then, with a quiet smile we return into the stillness of the Presence that will never complain about such a small matter. Smiling was so evidently created for our pleasure, so let us simply enjoy our inheritance, whatever our life situation, always realising that joy and sorrow are twins in the same womb we were birthed from.

NO PARLOUR TRICKS

Unhurriedly pursuing our journey into the realms of stillness and a total surrender to what is – rather than spending all our time wrestling to change things – can result in a remarkable difference to our life-style. As I mentioned earlier, many things may now seem to be working for us in quite a new way. In the stillness we sometimes experience times of bliss. At other times we strangely know what to do in situations that previously perplexed us. The 'still small voice' within becomes a reality and brings the assurance that all is well, whatever the outward appearances.

Not surprisingly, this happy state can bring its own temptations. Instead of becoming still because that is how we should be, we can aim to experience ecstasy as a kind of 'trip'. We can almost become 'stoned' on silence as a way of escaping the ordinary pressures of life that can often enlarge us. Such a seeking after experiences will not ensure lasting peace and joy. Rather, it will produce another performance-orientated activity that ends in a sad let-down sooner or later. Being still is being still; it does not have an end in view.

We may have read of advanced Masters who have performed incredible feats or miracles when in a deeply concentrated state. Some have ceased breathing and have been buried underground without harm for several days. Others have appeared in two places many miles apart within a few seconds, or perhaps simultaneously. On a seemingly lesser level, we may find that we ourselves are able to remain transfixed in a state of absolute stillness, living above our active mind realm, for very long periods of time.

Wonderful as such occurrences may appear, they are not a measure of spirituality. Living and loving, coping in the hurly-burly of everyday life, is the acid test of where we are really at – and having a still mind and a relaxed body will almost certainly lead us into those peaceful pastures. We are not in the business of performing parlour tricks to impress others, or even to impress ourselves. That is not the pathway of satisfaction.

Those of us who have seen supernatural happenings during our lifetime know that the memory of them fades sooner or later, and rightly so. We are not meant to dwell on the paranormal; we are meant to live happily in the here and now, accepting whatever it brings with equanimity. That is the miracle constantly performed in those who have learned the priceless worth of their interior life and who trust it above all else.

Let us continue our wholesome habit of pausing regularly to enjoy the spaciousness and silence that is always present, without looking for extraordinary happenings. Being still enough to enjoy the constant miracle of nature, working both within us and round about us, will be all we need to ensure a fulfilled journey throughout our sojourn here on earth. We shall not make a fuss or parade the details if remarkable things occasionally happen. It is the transcendent and immanent fellowship with the Unseen and Unheard which causes our hearts to warm and our eyes to sparkle. We shall have joined the increasing number of 'twinklers' who make such a difference to the daily lives of those they encounter. But we shall not be aware of that; we shall be just happily conscious of being fully alive.

AIDS TO LIVING

It may seem that I am advocating methods or techniques for coming to stillness and – in spite of my dislike of concepts – I must agree with you. However, let me emphasise that I do sense that one day all special means may cease. They are aids, not the real thing. That day will be when being still within ourselves is quite normal for us, when regular practice is no longer necessary. For most of us this process is gradual, no matter how impressive our initiation to stillness may have been.

The aids to a near-permanent state of relaxation and freedom from anxiety are many and varied. They can include the use of teaching or music tapes, or using a mantra – a repeated sound, word or phrase that causes us to focus more easily and without intensity. A candle may remind us that all things can be a sacrament, a means of grace.

Other helpful means are concentrating –

again without intensity – on our breath and our physical body, or being aware of the silence and spaciousness around us and within us. If you feel you need additional help, considerable guidance is available and will come your way, and you will find that the shelves of the high street bookshops are rich with material.

My own background includes the increasing use of 'glossolalia' – the gift of unlearned tongues or languages gained in my previous Christian experience, but they are not limited to one religion. For myself, one of the most constant aids has been using the awareness of silence and spaciousness. Being quietly conscious of parts of my body has also been most helpful. Learning to 'float' has been of inestimable value. I understand that most people begin by having their eyes closed, but my own experience started with my eyes open, and now I use both means during the course of a day.

Thankfully, we cannot be dogmatic in this matter; the river of life will take its own twists and turns. Listening to the silence that

is always present beyond all the noise produced in our current society has been the
simplest and most rewarding practice for me,
but your experience may be quite different.
Yet I still commend silence with all my heart.
Listening to silence brings inner stillness. You
can start to listen to the silence *right now* if you
would like to.

Sit comfortably erect where you are,
gently close your eyes and listen
without intensity.

After a while you may open your
eyes slowly and move your head, also
slowly, while you look at the space
all around you in the house or the
garden – or maybe even in your
prison cell or hospital ward.

Do not examine anything; just
be aware of objects and the space
surrounding them.

Savour being there in the
moment.

This state of awareness is so
enjoyable that you may want to

practise it often during the day, and certainly at the start and the end of the day, even if only for a few moments at a time.

Many might say I have been writing about the subject of meditation. However, I have an aversion to using such a word, for I have found it is sometimes greatly misunderstood and often causes prejudice to arise. Indeed, life for some has become just another 'subject' to be studied or problem to be solved, but that will never bring heartfelt contentment. Life is a mystery to be explored, and we are quite content for it to be so. We shall not constantly look for answers.

That most gifted teacher and author, Eckhart Tolle, uses the term 'sane living', and this is the best expression I have ever heard to indicate the whole experience of learning to have a quiet but increasingly alert mind. Given time, our stilled emotions and healthier bodies will often bear witness to our improved mind condition or sane living.

However, we should not aim for these changes, but should just learn to look upon them as pleasant surprises along the way.

I leave you in the still presence of Another; one beyond description, but yet a silent comfort to all those whose dependence is upon the inner-life that lights everyone who comes into the world.

LISTEN TO THE SILENCE

I have emphasised the matter of silence quite strongly throughout this book. This is probably because silence has played such a major part in my own development, but I acknowledge again that there are other ways to arrive at inner stillness and each person must find their own best means.

When we speak of entering into silence, it is important to understand that we are not listening *for* the silence or trying to find something that is lost. The silence is always here, even when there is great activity outside of us and inside our own minds. Silence and noise can exist at the same time. Unless we understand this we shall find we are trying to quieten our insistent thoughts or change our physical circumstances in order to discover inner silence.

The storm may roar about us, but our innermost person is residing quietly in the still eye of the storm. It is no use trying to resist the storm by fighting our way out, for what we resist persists. That fact is certainly worth repeating for a moment of quiet contemplation:

What We resist persists.

We need to let this statement slowly sink into our senses. Realising such truth may well be the early beginnings of acceptance, or 'going with the flow', which is an experience so many people talk about, but so few are able to practice. Tensing up to fight our problems only intensifies things. We need an inner assurance of a higher power within us, waiting for us to stand aside.

There are times when we may well enjoy going to a peaceful place, or rising early to experience the quiet of the day before the bustle of daily life gets into gear. But the silence and stillness we seek can be realised in the here and now. Around our busy thoughts there is a spaciousness that can be located without intensity. The silence and that spaciousness are one.

They are always there. Just taking a moment to be aware of this, if only for a few seconds, brings instant inner stillness and peace.

Let's not be ambitious and upset if our experience lasts such a short time, but let's be grateful, and then be fully conscious again whenever we want to. The old adversary, 'performance orientation', is always ready to whisper that our silence didn't last long, but we can observe the puffy cloud of such thought and just let it pass us by. Accusing voices never help us. In time we learn to smile at them and let our silence co-exist with them. Allowing more time to pass, we find we are increasingly being consciously present in this moment and enjoying a 'better standard of living' in the truest sense.

Since a child I have known the adage, 'Great oaks from little acorns grow', and maybe you have too. It can be helpful to pause each time we pass such a tree and remember the miracle of how so much came out of so little. But it took time, and the oak was all right at every stage of its growth; there was nothing wrong with it at all, it just wasn't very big for quite a while. It was perfect all the time and so are we; we're just unaware of it, that is all, and our behaviour has followed that unawareness. We can be still every now and again to realise that we are growing up into an awareness of what is already true in our innermost person.

As we read very slowly on, once again we make our pausing quite deliberate.

The silence and the spaciousness are all around us and within us.

We are not trying to have some great experience, but just simply pausing.

We can accompany this by being conscious of our slightly deeper breathing.

There is no hurry. We are not trying to understand anything very deep. We are relaxed.

We are aware of our arms and legs; they are heavy and they are warm.

We are aware of our chest. Our breathing is deep and even. Our heartbeat is slower.

We are being still. In this moment we are at peace. We will remain here awhile.

Whatever has been going on around us or within us, for just a few minutes we have been accepting the noise and allowing the surrounding silence to make its impression upon us. We have been *seeing through* all that is around us and *hearing past* any noise. We have been relaxing, not trying to do anything. We have been *aware* for a short while. To recall our earlier example, we have been counting ourselves 'dead' to all the busy noise and activity around us and in our minds. We shall reckon on what we now know is ultimately true – that the silence and stillness are there, in spite of all the evidence seemingly being against this. Without effort we shall continue to welcome the silence whenever it occurs to us to do so.

We are pleased with even a short taste of this restful condition, and are not out to break any records. More and more each day, we can simply pause from our activities and focus on nothing in particular. Again, it may help to move our heads slowly as we do this, as we vaguely scan whatever is in our vision. We are not naming what we are seeing, but *seeing through* once more and allowing ourselves to become aware of the silence. We are alert, but without any intensity. At any time, if we feel we are becoming hurried, then we can decide to pause and change the pace of our life at that moment. I often deliberately pause when I am in traffic that has slowed to a standstill and stress is near at hand, or when shaving, something I tend to hurry through because I do not naturally enjoy the morning ritual. It is always rewarding to observe myself in the mirror, simply having a pause and automatically beginning to breathe more deeply. A slight smile invariably appears without any effort to make it happen.

If we learn a new way of living in these little things of life, then the bigger things will

in time take care of themselves. We are prac-
tising the presence of the Eternal realm that
goes silently on, unaffected by the mêlée of
the busy world situation we may be engaged
in. Given more time, we shall become less and
less affected by constant pressure; our lives
will be evidently still and we will be consciously here in this present moment. Regrets
of the past and worries for the future begin to
drop away. We are fully alive. If we are not
busy, but have time on our hands, instead of
scurrying around finding things to do, we can
sit or lie still, or perhaps stroll very slowly, just
being aware of the miracles all around us.

If you feel like doing so, maybe it would
be good to read this chapter through again.
Even more slowly.

EVERYTHING IS

When the two words 'everything is' rose up within me at the close of a one-hour lying relaxation, they brought a deep feeling of well-being. I didn't want to move, but my breakfast was ready. That sense of stillness has not left me several hours later, so I have come to the word processor to see if I am meant to write some words.

Writing soon is not always a good thing to do, because it can lead to passing something on to others before it is a constant, abiding reality in one's own being. There is a risk that, in rushing to give the experience away too quickly, it may be lost to the bearer. Valuable things need to be treasured for their own sake. However, I am taking the risk today and maybe doing so will increase my understanding also.

I imagined the immediate question in many people's minds would probably be,

'Everything is *what?*', although that question never arose in my case. I somehow knew inwardly that the short sentence was complete in itself. Perhaps the way the words presented themselves encouraged me to italicise the third-person singular present of the verb to be: *is*.

That is it, isn't it? Everything just *is*. Even contemplating the statement makes me want to relax more, gently extend my arms a little and open my palms; to take my hands off life and to let it be. It is impossible to hold on to anything with our palms open and it seems symbolic of possessing nothing, yet strangely then having all things. We can enjoy everything without fear of it being stolen or damaged. Even pain and loss can be appreciated and add value to our lives, like an authentic dent of experience on a genuine piece of antique furniture.

I had never really understood the ancient mystics when they spoke of 'isness'. Not until this experience took me by surprise. Oh, I knew about it, had heard the word many times, but now it had become an integral part of the substance of my being and I felt totally comfortable with it there. 'Everything is, everything is, everything is.' I was able to savour the words without need of explanation. I was not considering the philosophical theory of existentialism, but something had happened to me and it can never un-happen.

For experience to radically change our lives, we need to be locked up into dependence upon revelation from a much higher source. That way no-one is at a disadvantage; professors and unlearned folk alike have access to the mind of the universe, which never was and never will be, but always is.

Everything is. We don't need the italics now. We are – and we know we are – part of the is.

GO CARELESSLY

With advancing years a few of my friends have taken on riverbank names (from *The Wind in the Willows* by Kenneth Grahame). I suppose it all started with my selection of an email address – 'molesmith@...' – and it was not long before Toad, Ratty and Badger had turned up. A friendly Hedgehog accepted our invitation to chat, and we even found that Rupert had strolled along the riverbank, elegantly resplendent in check trousers and a careless scarf. We let him stay because he is such a stylish bear!

All these dear animals have been released from the intensity of worshipping success and accuracy. They are free from public opinion and able to be uninhibitedly foolish. Well, most of the time. Toad initiated the signing-off line, 'Go carelessly', when corresponding with his friends along the bank. Some years ago another of our friends, who likes to be called

Owl, wrote a delightful song with the title 'I don't care!' This, of course, was severely misunderstood by many of the establishment, even though based on the words of Jesus when he exhorted his friends to 'be careful for nothing'. We need ears to hear aright, and that probably means being free from pedantic attitudes and so able to hear what the heart is saying.

As a rather feeble mole, I remember running into trouble with a tough rugby-playing friend in Holland when I casually remarked, 'Well, nothing matters, does it?' He retorted swiftly, 'It would matter if I punched you on the nose!' He is a great chap and was soon able to see that I meant, 'Nothing *really* matters, in ultimate terms' – or, to steal the famous words of Dame Julian of Norwich, 'All shall be well and all manner of thing shall be well.'

I am not advocating slipshod careless-ness, just a relaxed approach to life, being rid of all the intensity, accepting this moment as it is, whether it brings pain or pleasant sur-prises. Of course, we do not choose pain, but we don't *really* care which it is; *ultimately* it does not matter.

Some years ago Toad found a translation of a verse in Psalm 46 which said, 'Relax and know that I am God', and we all responded heartily. 'I knew it would be there somewhere,' quipped the mischievous creature. Surely, deep down, we all know it is better to relax than to struggle and strive. Getting a glimpse of the mysterious insight that somehow …

everything is intermingling for our eventual good

can begin to bring a more relaxed approach into the turmoil around us and within us, as the ever-increasing pace of life at the start of the twenty-first century threatens to gobble us up.

Can we just be still for a few final moments together and give that liberating insight a chance to embrace us? Reason will certainly not produce it, but as we rest our over-active minds, then the sense of divine presence or consciousness just might. If not, then maybe, when the time is right, it will steal up on us. However …

We can still breathe deeply right now

and begin to relax and pause once again. It is a very wholesome habit.

As we have travelled together through the pages of this little book, it has been my constant hope that the lack of intensity will prove infectious. I am not hopeful that a mole of very little left-hand brain will impart much intellectual content, but I am hopeful that the peace I have found, and my contentment with things as they are, will rub off … if you are not careful!

Appendix

What about religion in all this? For those who have been used to the practice of prayer, it may come as a surprise to be *still* and not to ask for anything or continually pour out our troubles. In my experience, words became redundant and I felt compelled to stop using them. Now I feel drawn simply to bring others with me into the sense of stillness – call it the presence of God, if that is more comfortable for you – a practice that has been richly rewarding.

For much of my long life I have been known as a Christian, although frankly I do not feel the need of a label at all. I am not this or that; I am simply Maurice, someone who does not firmly hold a set of beliefs, but someone who knows only what he has experienced.

During my years inside a structured religious system it seemed there was always

an 'us' and 'them' situation, and this was
determined by what we each did or did not
believe from Scripture. However, one of the
statements attributed to Jesus kept unsettling
me. It was, 'By their fruits you shall know
them.' I finally had to acknowledge that I
could see as much – and sometimes more –
'fruit' in the lives of people of other religions,
or those of none at all.

Happily, this dilemma was fully resolved
for me when I eventually ceased to label and
pass judgement on others. People can believe
whatever they like as long as they don't try to
convert me to their way of thinking. If our
living is attractive enough, then others will be
drawn to find out what is behind it. Probably
that is not a very satisfying explanation for
many, but in my experience it is a far more
satisfying way of living.

Do I now miss my attendance at church
(temple, tabernacle or mosque) services?
Frankly, I do not. Although the buildings can
be undeniably beautiful and even inspiring,
they have never been very important to
me, and several decades of meetings have

certainly been more than enough. I felt the 'church' has always been the people themselves, not the meeting-place or the fact of congregating in large numbers. I somehow always knew that I would never lose my true friends or genuine relationships whether I attended a place of worship or not.

Many years ago I spontaneously coined the term 'the nebulous church' – my description for our life-involvement with people that is always evolving, a part of the constant change that is here to stay. We just cannot pin it down. This is how I live, but it is not necessarily how I feel you should live. Confronted by a question on the matter of preferences, one of the Sisters of Mary once answered delightfully, 'Whatever is your joy.' And that is an expression that fits me comfortably. Of course I have my feelings about religious practices, but they are not worth taking issue over. Loving one another and appreciating whatever we can at all times, is a far more constructive and less divisive emphasis, or so it seems to me.

Dogmatic belief in the exact words of the

scriptures of any religion has always seemed to me to be unhelpful, to say the least, and often it obscures a truer meaning. A small example from my past history: I always had trouble with the New Testament words, 'Love believes *all things*'. It was just impossible for me to swallow, until one day I discovered a new interpretation – an approach I find more helpful than rigid translation – that read, 'Love puts the best possible construction on everything.' Love believes the best? This rang completely true to me and all confusion was quickly dispelled.

If we cannot agree about these matters, then that is fine and I quite happily reiterate, 'Whatever is your joy.' I suppose some will stay in their religious systems, others will leave them. Some may never want to join anything at all. Let us to our own selves be true and love all of mankind for all of our days.

Whoever you are, whatever you believe or don't believe, I can only conclude by once again gently encouraging you to be still, both now and often. Then once again, let time pass and consciously experience what follows.